THE SUTTON L

Life as a

Victorian

Lady

Pamela Horn

SUTTON PUBLISHING

Sutton Publishing Limited
Phoenix Mill · Thrupp · Stroud
Gloucestershire · GL5 2BU

First published 2007

British Library Cataloguing in Publication Data
A catalogue for this book is available from the British Library.

ISBN 978-0-7509-4607-0

Typeset in Bembo.
Typesetting and origination by
Sutton Publishing Limited.
Printed and bound in England.

Contents

To my husband, who has helped in so many
different ways

Shillings and Pence Conversion Table

Old money	Decimal	Old money	Decimal
1*d*	½p	1*s* 7*d*	8p
2*d* or 3*d*	1p	1*s* 8*d*	8½p
4*d*	1½p	1*s* 9*d* or 1*s* 10*d*	9p
5*d*	2p	1*s* 11*d*	9½p
6*d*	2½p	2*s*	10p
1*s*	5p	2*s* 6*d*	12½p
1*s* 1*d*	5½p	3*s*	15p
1*s* 2*d* or 1*s* 3*d*	6p	5*s*	25p
1*s* 6*d*	7½p	20*s*	100p, i.e. £1

CHAPTER 1

Introduction

From a twenty-first century perspective, the lives of Victorian ladies appear privileged and comfortable, cushioned against the harsher realities of life. Domestic staff performed much of the drudgery associated with household chores, and left mistresses time to enjoy leisure pursuits. Most were expected to find personal fulfilment within the home, as wives and mothers and as hostesses dispensing hospitality to guests. In 1855, the Revd Charles Kingsley in a *Lecture to Ladies* declared that a woman's 'first duties [were] to her own family, her own servants'.

It was women who made the 'ordinances and regulations' that governed polite society, through their power to give or withhold invitations and to choose on whom they would call or from whom they would receive calls. As the contemporary journal the *Lady's Companion* commented on 10 March 1900, while the male members of high society were willing to associate with an ill-educated millionaire, that was unlikely to apply to their female relatives. These would not visit the wife and daughter of such a man, or receive them in their home, if they lacked 'refinement and culture. The penniless daughter of an underpaid curate would (provided she were a gentlewoman) have the entrée into houses that would resolutely close their doors on the pretensions of the millionaire's family'.

It was to advise the socially inept on possible pitfalls that books of etiquette proliferated in the second half of the nineteenth century. In 1866, for example, *Etiquette for Ladies* pointed out that in conversation 'the voice of a lady is . . . always low and nicely modulated'. A provincial accent was to be avoided and the vocabulary carefully chosen to exclude words and expressions deemed vulgar in the 'best' circles. 'Don't utter exclamations such as "My!" . . . They are VERY vulgar', it warned. Vulgarity, ostentatious conduct and conspicuous attire were to be eschewed at all costs, as was any involvement in public scandal. That included marital infidelity. When Lady Aylesford was divorced in 1878 on account of her adultery with Lord Blandford, her name was struck from guest lists and she was 'cut' in public. Interestingly, Lord Blandford suffered no such social sanctions.

Within the household, the general preoccupation with status and hierarchy was reflected in the way that the accommodation itself was divided among family members, guests and the domestic staff. Each had their own quarters, with the servants residing in the basement or the attics or in a separate wing, while the nursery and schoolroom were also located at the top of the house, where the noise of the children would not disturb the rest of the family. Many of the main rooms were split along gender lines, so that the morning-room, boudoir and drawing-room were regarded as female territory, while the library, study and smoking room belonged to the menfolk. As far as possible the servants were to remain out of sight as they went about their duties, by the use of a system of backstairs and back corridors. In this way family privacy would be preserved.

The concern about status and propriety also extended to what was seen as the appropriate attire for domestic staff. In April 1840 Anne Sturges Bourne, who lived on a small Hampshire estate, admitted to a friend that her mother was very unhappy 'abt. housemaids' bonnet caps & brooches, & the difficulty of drawing a line of what is smart & what plain'. But she recognised that when it came 'to a struggle of how much the maid may presume or the mistress forbid, there is little good done, & they wear smart things by stealth'.

Young unmarried girls were expected to be chaperoned when they went into public places or attended social functions. Hence Lucy Lyttelton, daughter of the 4th Lord Lyttelton, felt 'suddenly . . . scampish' when in April 1861, at the age of about 20, she walked alone on the pier at Brighton. Two days later she attended an afternoon church service in the resort and 'having to walk back alone, I pretended to belong to two elderly ladies in succession, who I don't think found out they were escorting me'. Even in the mid-1890s the newly married American-born Duchess of Marlborough was surprised to discover it was considered improper for an English lady to walk alone in Piccadilly and in Bond Street, or to be seen in a hansom cab, while 'to visit a music-hall was out of the question'.

Gender differences applied, too, with boys being preferred to girls, especially in landed families. Lady Maud Cecil, oldest child of the 3rd Marquess of Salisbury, was 'very much offended' when at the age of 3, shortly after the birth of her eldest brother, she overheard 'people say when addressing the baby, "It is a good thing it *was* a boy this time"'. From that time, she added drily, 'I began to look at life from a feminist standpoint.'

It was part of the same process that married women were expected to defer to their husbands when it came to taking decisions, although that did not always apply in practice. Independent-minded women, like Clara Paget, wife of a physician and teacher of medicine at Cambridge University, 'managed' both the male and female members of her family and looked after money matters. When she was away in Wales pursuing her antiquarian interests she sent instructions to her daughters in Cambridge by letter on how they should proceed. Clergy wives often shared in their husbands' parish duties, holding mothers' meetings, running clothing and coal clubs, and teaching in Sunday school.

Marriage was regarded as the only acceptable career for a gentlewoman, since paid employment was considered impossible if genteel status were to be maintained. The underlying attitude was made clear by a contributor to the *Englishwoman's Journal* of 1866: 'My opinion is that if a woman is obliged to work, at once ... she loses that peculiar position which the word *lady* conventionally designates.' Occasional sums might be earned, perhaps by writing articles for periodicals, but regular remuneration was out of the question. Only those spinsters fortunate enough to inherit a fortune or to be asked to manage the household of an unmarried brother or widowed father escaped the stigma of being regarded as marginalised nonentities, or mere 'old maids', when they reached middle age.

It was against this restricted view of the female role that Florence Nightingale railed bitterly when in the early 1850s she wrote of women who were

never supposed to have any occupation of sufficient importance *not* to be interrupted . . . and have trained themselves so as to consider whatever they do as *not* of such value to the world or to others, but that they can throw it up at the first 'claim of social life'. They have accustomed themselves to consider intellectual occupation as a merely selfish amusement which it is their 'duty' to give up for every trifler more selfish than themselves.

She herself escaped from that limited life shortly afterwards when she took up her nursing career. Perhaps fortunately, few other single women felt as strongly as she did about their narrow prospects.

Within this general framework, therefore, many Victorian ladies led a sheltered existence. But that did not mean that they were idle. Apart from performing their social duties, paying calls, writing letters, making visits, attending parties, balls, the theatre and art galleries, and visiting their dressmakers, mothers and older sisters often gave lessons to the younger children and, most importantly, wives supervised the smooth running of the household. They also did needlework, sketched, read, and played the piano, and within the limits of a restricted education, cultivated their character, mind and abilities to benefit those around them. Nearly all engaged in charitable work, often acting as links between rich and poor through their role as dispensers of aid to the needy. Margaret, Countess of Jersey, once told a friend wryly that the most appropriate epitaph for her tombstone would be, 'She Gave Away Prizes'. But most women welcomed the opportunity to help and to be useful.

Lady Colin Campbell, writing in 1893, noted other desirable attributes:

A true lady will be quite natural and easy in her manners, and this will have the effect of putting those at their ease who are in her company, whatever their station in life may be. She will shrink from all affectation and avoid all pretension, and never try, by any means, to appear other than she really is . . . A quiet dignity will pervade all her actions.

Strong religious convictions and the exercise of moral influence were further characteristics of

Victorian ladyhood. Such influence included the holding of daily family prayers, frequent attendance at church services, and, in some cases, a recognition of personal sinfulness, or what was considered sinfulness, and a constant struggle against it. This was true of the daughters of Lady Claud Hamilton, who suffered deep anxieties during their youth. In the autumn of 1863, 16-year-old Emma confessed that she would 'like to go among the poor more now, to do good . . . But I am not fit to do the least thing in God's service while I am so wicked myself, but I think if I could venture to give bibles, it might not be too presumptious.' A little later her sister, Louisa, aged 22, admitted that when the family left Elton, their Cambridgeshire home, she had 'made a strong resolution to get ready for death . . . Surely we ought all to live in a constant state of readiness for death – living each day as if the last, making use of every . . . moment to send before us more treasures of good works.' Despite her forebodings, Louisa married in 1876 and lived to a ripe old age.

Fortunately, the piety of most Victorian ladies was less gloomy than this.

Moral influence was important, too. In *Castle Richmond* (1860), Anthony Trollope commented on the necessity of having a female to head the domestic arrangements of a household because of the steadying and moralising effect of 'tea and small talk' on its other members. Hence in June 1853 the widowed Lady Carnarvon advised her teenage second son to avoid such 'ungentlemanlike, barbarous and corrupting' pastimes as 'ratting' and 'ferreting': 'there is always something very degrading to the mind when *Man* the master spirit *looks on* applauding & encouraging two *lower* animals to tear each other to pieces'. That did not apply to hunting and shooting since there 'Man . . . takes his *share* in the sport . . . the animal has a chance of escape and has the liberty of employing in self defence the powers given to him for that very purpose by his creator.' Nevertheless, her son should 'not allow [his] new friend the gun to occupy too much . . .

very precious time' and divert him from his other duties.

Not until the Victorian era was drawing to an end was there some loosening of the restrictions on female activities, as a small number of girls from genteel families began to enter higher education and to travel around unchaperoned, especially when engaged in charitable work. For older women, transport improvements, such as quicker trains and the construction of the underground railway in London, as well as the opening of department stores and tea rooms, made independent shopping trips attractive. As the *Lady's World* advised in 1886, readers could easily travel between London and Bath and back in a day in order to visit the capital: 'This is no small advantage when you have a day's shopping to get through, or winter gowns and mantles to be tried on at your favourite London modiste's.' Even in the 1870s Mrs Jebb went to London for a day's shopping by train from Cambridge, a journey of over 50 miles each way.

However, the cosseted existence of some of the younger women caused frustration among the more thoughtful. Cynthia Charteris, the future Lady Cynthia Asquith, summarised their feelings at the close of the century:

Our helplessness equalled our want of independence . . . Everything was done for us. I was never so much as taught how to mend or wash – let alone make – my clothes. I couldn't even pack for myself. Of cooking I knew no more than of the art of navigation . . . A woman who can't cook is a hopeless cripple at the mercy of anyone who can.

Yet it is important to remember that women's varying personalities – the assertiveness, self-assurance and arrogance of some, and the timidity or frivolity of others – undermine any view of Victorian ladies as uniformly demure and obedient, no matter how rigid society's rules might be.

CHAPTER 2

Growing Up

It was during the first two years of marriage that most upper-class women became pregnant and, especially in the case of landed families, there was pressure on them to produce a male heir as soon as possible. Early in 1896 the newly married Duchess of Marlborough remembered her first meeting with her husband's formidable grandmother, a few months after her wedding. Following 'an embarrassing inspection of my person', she fixed her cold grey eyes on the young Duchess and announced: 'Your first duty is to have a child and it must be a son . . . Are you in the family way?' Feeling crushed and depressed by the encounter, she was glad to take her leave. In the event, her first son was born in September 1897, but those women who failed to bear a child felt this as a blot on their femininity. It could cause much unhappiness, as in the case of Lady Frederick Cavendish (the former Lucy Lyttelton). In February 1866 she attended two 'pretty baptisms' and was moved to tears, 'so foolishly did I long to see a baby of our own christened'. This was after about eighteen months of marriage; however, she was destined to remain childless.

In the early and mid-Victorian years wives, even in the 'best' circles, often had large families, at a time when both maternal and infant mortality were at high levels. Puerperal fever was a particular danger for new mothers, and the diary of Lady Frederick Cavendish is littered with references to friends who had died or suffered serious illness as a result of a confinement that had gone wrong. On 11 December 1866 she noted: 'A terribly sad thing has happened: the death of Lady Fortescue in her confinement, leaving 13 children the eldest only 18.' Lucy's own mother died in 1857, a few months after bearing her twelfth child in less than twenty years of marriage. She was only 44 and her two eldest daughters, Meriel and Lucy, had to try to take her place with the younger children. Towards the end of the century contraception became more widely accepted and family size consequently was reduced.

When a baby was born, much of the responsibility for its care was handed over to nursery staff, although the extent to which this happened depended on the mother's attitude. When Lady Ridley had her first two children in the early 1840s she not only breastfed them (as was customary at that time) but anxiously consulted her mother about the best way to look after them, even though she had a full-time nanny. Lady Leconfield wrote almost daily to her children's nurse when she was away from the family estate at Petworth, and received detailed accounts of their health and progress. She and the nurse were mutually concerned with the children's welfare and her letters were eagerly awaited in the nursery. When they were ill she helped to look after them.

However, in many cases children were brought up by the nurse until they reached the age of 5 or 6, when they began to have lessons with a governess in the schoolroom. Nurses not only had physical care of them but taught them good personal habits and manners. Often they became part of their charges' emotional life. Violet Maxse, whose parents separated when she was 5, regarded her nurse, Emma, as 'the keystone of our family arch'.

Nursery meals were plain and monotonous and were prepared separately from those for the rest of the household. Even in affluent families children were frequently dressed in simple, hand-me-down clothes. Although Frances Maynard, the future Countess of Warwick, had inherited a large estate at the age of 3, she spent her childhood in frocks cut down from her mother's cast-off dresses, 'so that they might not be too elegant for a young girl'. Toys were, however, usually plentiful and large gardens enabled children to play and romp in safety. Many had pets.

Mothers or older sisters sometimes gave lessons to the younger children, as Lady Leconfield did. She also played games with them and took them for walks. But governesses were recruited, too, perhaps to free a mother's time for other activities or to bring expertise unavailable in the family. Molly Bell, the daughter of a wealthy Teesside ironmaster, remembered with pleasure the music and French lessons given to her and her sister by their mother, and the history teaching of their stepsister, Gertrude. But the instruction provided by the governess was uninspiring. 'For more than ten years I was bored all the time,' she wrote later. On occasion, specialist teachers were brought in to give music and dancing lessons, or the girls attended outside classes. Gwen Raverat, the daughter of a Cambridge professor, remembered the drawing class she attended each week as 'the centre of [her] youthful existence', while the teaching given by a series of governesses was 'stupid' and uninteresting.

Lessons were normally held in a domestic setting and rarely extended beyond 'accomplishments' such as foreign languages, music, sketching and dancing, plus the 'basics' of reading, writing, simple arithmetic and religion. Mabell Gore, daughter of Lord and Lady Sudley, was brought up by a stern and very pious grandmother after her mother died when the little girl was 4. The grandmother encouraged no worldly ambitions in Mabell and her two younger sisters; indeed, their lives were to be based on religious duties and good works. Mabell subsequently described her education as 'deplorable. We learned dancing and what was called "deportment" from the best teachers, and riding in the fashionable Curzon Equestrian School. . . . For the rest we depended on the inevitable governess who imparted to us a smattering of the limited range of subjects considered sufficient for girls of our generation.' Mabell's desire to study science and mathematics was rejected as 'unfeminine' and her clandestine efforts to learn the Greek alphabet were quickly thwarted. She was 'ordered to do some needlework instead'.

A minority of girls overcame the limitations of their schooling by embarking on a programme of self-education as they grew older, but such undirected learning was often ineffectual. Although new girls' schools had been established by this time, they were rarely attended by the daughters of upper- or upper-middle-class families. Gwen Raverat remembered a peeress of her acquaintance who pronounced magisterially: '*We* do not send our daughters away to school.' Occasionally parents from a professional background, valuing education for its own sake, might take advantage of the new opportunities. Margaret Gladstone, the daughter of a chemistry professor in London and later the wife of the Labour Prime Minister, Ramsay MacDonald, attended for five years at Doreck College in London during the 1880s, before moving on to 'the Ladies' Classes' at King's College for several more years. There she studied physiology, Greek, moral philosophy, architecture and ethics, as well as more traditional female subjects such as modern European languages.

Elizabeth Haldane, born in 1862 into a distinguished Scottish academic family, found another solution. She lost her father when she was 15, and she and her mother lived frugally in the country so that her brothers could be 'set up for life'. She would have liked to go to college, but that was impossible. Instead she organised a rigorous programme of self-education through correspondence courses, with the encouragement of her mother and aunts, who were enthusiastic feminists.

In other cases well-to-do girls went for a year or so to a French or Swiss finishing school, which normally offered the customary range of 'accomplishments', or they travelled on the Continent. Great importance was attached to fluency in French. When 4-year-old Nancy Mitford was taken to see the strong-minded Blanche, Countess of Airlie, who was a distant relative, the old lady asked, 'How is the child progressing in French?' When Nancy's mother confessed the little girl had not begun to study the language, the Countess replied in an 'awful' voice, 'There is nothing so inferior as a gentlewoman who has no French.' The result was that 'Mlle Séréza, the only person who brought a civilizing influence to my childhood, always spent the summer holidays with us.'

A few girls, as they grew older, developed their accomplishments to a high standard, becoming competent musicians, skilled artists, or fluent linguists; but most remained mediocre performers.

During their early years these girls also began to distribute charity, in preparation for their future role as a 'Lady Bountiful'. They accompanied their mothers on visits to the poor and were assigned tasks of their own, sewing baby clothes and flannel petticoats, or trotting from door to door with soup and moral tracts.

During the normal daily routine mothers frequently spent only a brief period with their offspring, usually around tea-time, when the children were brought to the drawing-room for about an hour by their nurse. A mother's social duties were considered sufficiently important to preclude greater intimacy.

However, at a time when family ties were strong there were long visits to cousins and other relatives. This was the case with the Lytteltons and their Gladstone cousins, with cavalcades of nurses and children travelling between the Lyttelton home, Hagley, and Hawarden and London, where the Gladstones lived. In January 1857, when there were eighteen youngsters staying at Hagley, Lucy Lyttelton described the house as 'choked, overflowing, echoing with children'.

Once they reached the age of 17 or 18, the lives of these young gentlewomen changed, as they 'came out' into adult society, putting up their hair, lengthening their skirts and acquiring a fashionable wardrobe. Early in the twentieth century Gwen Raverat ruefully recalled that when she was 18 her skirts came down to the ground, while Sunday dresses had to have a little train behind. 'It was difficult to walk freely in the heavy tweed "walking skirts", which kept on catching between the knees.' Hems became muddy in wet weather, and as respectable young ladies they had to have their head covered when out of doors: 'the hat was an essential part of dress'. The transition from schoolroom to adult world, with its balls, banquets, country house visits and sporting events, was of great importance. As a contemporary magazine, the *Lady's Newspaper*, warned, a girl's 'prospects of marriage, even her entire future, [might] well depend upon her conduct at this most important juncture of her Youth'. A false step could prove disastrous.

Not surprisingly, many debutantes found their first entry into grown-up society a nerve-racking experience. It was 'uncontrollable panic' that caused Gwen Raverat to upset a dish of spinach into her lap at one of her first dinner parties. 'I felt sick for several days before my first dances, for fear I should be shamed in public, by not having enough partners.' Over time most of these anxieties disappeared.

For those in the upper ranks of society, 'coming out' involved the ritual of presentation at Court, although this might be preceded by a round of visits to relatives, to accustom them to adult life after the limitations of the schoolroom. That was true of Lucy Lyttelton, who remembered visiting the home of a cousin, Lady Wenlock, with her father and elder sister. There she played cards for money for the first time and enjoyed the musical evenings.

Presentation at Court took place at one of the official drawing rooms, presided over by Queen Victoria. Without this, declared *Etiquette for Ladies* (1900), 'a girl has no recognised position. . . . Prior to this important function, she is a "juvenile", but after making her profound curtsey to Royalty she leaves the magic presence a "grown up!"' During the final twenty years of the Queen's reign the number of presentations more than doubled, necessitating the addition of a fourth drawing room in 1880, instead of the previous three, and a fifth in 1895.

Molly Bell took part in her first London Season in 1899, at the age of 17. 'To those who had any pretentions to be in Society, with a big S,' she wrote later, 'it was essential to be presented at Court.' Usually a mother presented her daughter or, as in the case of Lucy Lyttelton, whose mother was dead, the role would be taken by another relative or older married friend.

Molly remembered the ritual involved:

To don an evening dress in the middle of a March morning was enough to make the stoutest shiver . . . I wore a white satin dress covered with a tunic of tulle, with little bunches of lilies of the valley sewn on to the skirt at intervals. My train . . . hung from the shoulders where it was firmly attached with hooks and eyes. In my hair I wore three white ostrich feathers, small and tightly curled . . . together

with a veil of white net, a yard and a half long . . .
My train was three yards long, as prescribed by the
official regulation for ladies' Court dress.

When their carriage reached St James's Park, it was
'absorbed into a crowd of other landaus and
broughams, all bound for the same place'. The presentation began at 3 p.m. and as no refreshments were
provided at a drawing room, it was 'a great relief to get
home and have tea, to which many of our friends
came, to admire our dresses and to hear how we had
comported ourselves'.

Molly enjoyed the subsequent social round,
including the fun of going to parties. But it was not all
frivolity. 'I practised three or four hours a day on the
piano, I went regularly to my choral societies, I
embroidered fire screens, I went to museums, I read
solid books, and found life enormously interesting.'

At this stage, care was taken to ensure that the girls
met only the 'right' people, so that if and when they

married, it was to a suitable spouse. For mothers, it was a time of some anxiety, with much ingenuity and energy devoted to this subtle form of social – and marital – control. 'Most ladies', comments Victoria Glendinning, 'did not feel they were wasting their time paying morning calls, giving "At Homes", chaperoning their daughters at balls, working out who should go down to dinner with whom . . . This was their work, and their duty.'

CHAPTER 3

Etiquette and the Social Round

'Etiquette is a subject of universal importance, for it furnishes a guide to the regulation of conduct. Every social event is governed by certain laws, a knowledge of which saves all occasion for doubts,' declared the advice book *Etiquette for Ladies and Gentlemen* in 1894. It was a code that had evolved particularly from the 1820s, as the number of families engaged in polite society, and especially in the London Season, increased from perhaps three or four hundred at the beginning of the nineteenth century to over ten times that number at its end. It was a system designed to shield the elite from what an 1830s social guide called 'the intrusion of the impertinent, the improper, and the vulgar'.

The rituals covered such matters as the making of formal calls, the leaving of visiting cards, the securing of introductions, the necessity for young, unmarried gentlewomen to be chaperoned, and the question of precedence on social occasions such as dinner parties. Formal morning calls, for example, were always made *after* luncheon (Lady Colin Campbell suggested between 3 p.m. and 6 p.m.) and ought never to last longer than 15 or 20 minutes. According to Mrs Beeton's *Book of Household Management* (1861), they should be made after dining at a friend's house or after a ball, picnic or other party. During a call a lady would not remove her bonnet or outer clothing. Mrs Beeton also advised that a 'strict account should be kept of ceremonial visits, and notice [taken] how soon your visits have been returned. An opinion may thus be formed as to whether your frequent visits are . . . desirable.'

To Lady Colin Campbell these 'visits of form' were the basis on which that great structure, society, rests. You cannot invite people to your house, however often you may have met them elsewhere, until you have first called upon them in a formal manner, and they have returned the visit. It is a kind of safeguard against any acquaintances which are thought to be undesirable. If you do not wish to continue the friendship, you discontinue to call.

On all such occasions, cards must be left and should the lady upon whom the call was made 'not be at home, you turn down one corner of the cards, which signifies that you have called personally'. When making these visits it was essential to engage in 'small talk', which should never degenerate into mere gossip.

In some cases the mistress of a household would designate particular days on which she was 'At Home' to visitors, both formal callers and friends. But whereas the former would not be offered refreshments, the latter might be given afternoon tea.

In making introductions or in meeting acquaintances of a higher social rank, care had always to be taken. In such cases a lady of inferior status would await recognition by her social superior. Likewise, when issuing invitations to dinner parties or other events to persons of superior ranking, the hostess would 'request the honour' instead of 'pleasure' of their company, pronounced *Etiquette for Ladies* (1866).

The same social manual also warned that any violation of the 'order of precedency in going in to dinner' was 'likely to give offence', and this question should be settled by the 'lady of the house' well in advance. So important had the question become by the 1880s that Burke's Peerage published a *Book of Precedence*, in order to avoid embarrassing mistakes. Even 'Society' magazines like *The Queen* offered advice on social behaviour during that decade, and inexperienced hostesses might consult friends and relatives on the finer points of etiquette. In the 1890s the newly married Elinor Glyn, novelist wife of a minor Essex landowner, received guidance from Lady Warwick that while army or naval officers, diplomats and clergymen might be invited to luncheon or dinner, doctors and solicitors never were, though they might be asked to garden parties.

Nevertheless, even when care was taken, problems could arise. The Duchess of Marlborough spent hours in ensuring that the rules of precedence were strictly adhered to for guests at dinner parties. That applied not merely to seating arrangements but to the procession in to dinner. At her first big weekend house party she listed in order of precedence the four earls who were guests, only to be informed by one of them on the second evening that 'I had not given him precedence over Lord B. as I should have done'.

In Cambridge academic circles, the regular round of formal dinner parties was also important. Gwen Raverat claimed that guests were seated in accordance with long-established protocol, with the 'Heads of House ranking by the dates of the foundation of their colleges, except that the Vice-Chancellor would come first of all'. The process continued down 'all the steps of the hierarchy'. She then added, drily, that it was better not to invite 'too many important people at the same time, or the complications became insoluble' for hostesses of 'only ordinary culture . . . and some of the grandees were very touchy about their rights, and their wives were even more easily offended'.

It was in these circumstances that ladies of inferior rank received the attentions of social superiors with a degree of humility. This was true of Charlotte Phillimore, whose husband was a prominent legal figure. During the 1870s and 1880s her diaries mention visits to her home by the Earl of Carnarvon in effusive terms, as in October 1877:

> Lord C. very pleasant and courteous as always, liked my pair of Highclere sketches [Highclere Castle was his Hampshire seat], said to me, 'I would give up my Secretary of Stateship to sketch as you do.'

A few months later when he and his sister dined with the Phillimores, she noted with gratification that Lord Carnarvon had 'ordered some salad plates to be made for us because we had none'.

In households with large numbers of servants, strict rules also applied to them. That included the custom for the first footman to be regarded as the lady's footman. He would stand behind her chair at the dining table, and any chore the lady's maid required to have done for her mistress was his responsibility. When she went out driving he sat on the box with the coachman and would open and shut the door for her and, if necessary, wrap a fur rug round her knees.

Central to the pleasure-seeking world was the London Season itself. Those involved in politics returned to the capital in February to prepare for the new parliamentary session, but for other members of the social elite the Season began in April or May and lasted to July. After that came summer migrations to Cowes for the sailing and to the grouse moors for shooting, or to the seaside or the Continent for holidays. The Season's importance lay in its role in bringing together the country's leading families for social, political and marital contacts. According to Lady Randolph Churchill, in the 1880s so significant was it that 'no votary of fashion' would miss a week or a day. From early May a multiplicity of dinners, balls and parties succeeded one another, while there were concerts, operas and the theatre to attend, as well as sporting fixtures. A few racing people went to Newmarket for a week, but the 'fashionable world flocked only to the classic races – the Derby, Ascot and Goodwood'.

By the end of the century there were parties arranged at Hurlingham to watch the pigeon-shooting, at Ranelagh for polo, and at the Botanical Gardens, where fashionable flower shows were held. Another integral part of all this was Rotten Row, where each day between 12 noon and 2 p.m. the social elite met to ride, drive or walk and to converse with friends.

However, it was essential for young ladies to have a chaperon if they went riding or walking. The presence of a groom only was inadequate and 'open to objection', declared *The Manners of the Aristocracy by One of Themselves* (1881).

Participation in these social events involved many changes of costume. That applied also to the country house weekends associated with the London Season and its aftermath. The Duchess of Marlborough recalled the numerous outfits required for Blenheim Palace shooting parties in the 1890s. An elegant costume of velvet or silk was worn at breakfast. The men would then go off to their sport while the ladies read the newspapers and gossiped until it was time to join the guns for luncheon. For that they changed into tweeds. The meal was served in a lodge or a tent, and afterwards the ladies usually accompanied the menfolk to watch a drive or two, before returning home. An elaborate tea gown was then donned for tea, after which 'we played cards or listened to a Viennese band or to the organ until time to dress for dinner, when we again adorned ourselves in satin, or brocade, with a great display of jewels. All these changes necessitated a tremendous outlay, since one was not supposed to wear the same gown twice.'

Not all members of polite society found such events enjoyable. Mary Gladstone, daughter of the Prime Minister, was less than enchanted when she visited Waddesdon, home of Baron Ferdinand de Rothschild, in early August 1885. 'Felt much oppressed with the extreme gorgeousness and luxury . . . pottered about looking at calves, hothouses, everything laid out with immense care, some rather cockney things, rockeries and such like.' She admired the pictures in Baron Ferdinand's sitting room but noted disapprovingly that there was 'not a book in the house save 20 improper French novels'.

To Beatrice Potter, the intellectual daughter of a Gloucestershire country house family, the social whirl was an unwelcome distraction. 'After a dinner when I have talked, I am absolutely useless in the way of brain-work . . . in the society-life one leads in London one's little brain is for the most part engaged in chattering . . . Conversation becomes a mania and a most demoralizing one.'

Hostesses sought to ensure that important functions did not clash, but that was not always possible. In 1839, 19-year-old Cecilia Parke, whose father was a leading member of the judiciary, spent the spring and summer in a round of social engagements, which she attended with her mother. One evening they dined at Lord de Grey's, where there were twenty-two people,

many of whom came in in the middle of dinner, for his Lordship never waits a second for a single living creature . . . After the feast we went to a party at the Duchess of Roxburghe's where every snob in London was present. The poor Duchess is quite overwhelmed with her acquaintance . . . We went for a few minutes to an unknown lady called Mrs Douglas Holford, who had a nasty party of such ugly

people that Mama declared they were all masked . . .
We went to Lady Domville's – the nicest ball I have
been at this year.

There, she noted triumphantly, '33 people asked me to
dance'.

One of the purposes of the London Season was to
enable young unmarried gentlewomen such as Cecilia
Parke to meet a suitable husband. Some, like Lady
Warwick, were successful in their first Season. In June
1880 she became engaged to Lord Brooke, heir to the
Earl of Warwick. But for others there was a longer
wait. The strict chaperonage often inhibited the
development of romantic relationships. As Leonore
Davidoff has commented, the dowagers who set many
of Society's rules made it 'an extreme trial for a girl to
attempt an alternative path . . . there was a general but
personalized surveillance of every step she took'. Even
sitting on a sofa with a young man was regarded as
improper in some families.

Occasionally parents opposed a match because the correct courtship procedures had not been followed: they resented the lack of consultation more than they objected to the candidate. Equally, girls were expected to acquiesce when a suitable offer of marriage was made. Mary Glynne, who later became the wife of the 4th Lord Lyttelton, was reproved by an aunt when she refused Lord Gairlie's proposal. 'Women are not like men,' wrote the aunt, 'they cannot chuse, nor is it creditable or lady-like to be what is called in love.'

Girls who lacked a sizeable dowry found difficulty in making a good match. But too great an anxiety on the part of a potential spouse to marry for financial motives was frowned upon. In 1895 Lady Londonderry commented acidly on a bridegroom who had 'married the £10,000 a year as well as the lady'.

Before the Married Women's Property Acts of 1870 and 1882 brought about some security for the bride, well-to-do families often arranged a marriage settlement as part of their marital preparations to protect a daughter's monetary position. The intention was to limit a husband's right to dispose of any property that his wife had brought into the marriage. Under the 1870 legislation, women were permitted to retain property or earnings acquired after marriage; that of 1882 allowed them to keep possessions owned at the time of their marriage, without the need for a legal settlement. These changes particularly benefited upper-middle-class wives who had frequently lacked the safeguard of a marriage settlement because of the legal costs and the complex negotiations involved.

After marriage, there was the question of being accepted by the in-laws. During the 1860s, when the gregarious Lucy Lyttelton married Lord Frederick Cavendish, second son of the Duke of Devonshire, she found her taciturn father-in-law rather forbidding. Two years after the marriage a younger sister recorded that Lucy was 'still rather on pins and needles with the Duke'. Mabell Gore, after marrying the Earl of Airlie, experienced similar difficulties with her mother-in-law.

The dowager countess still lived at the family seat, Cortachy, and controlled the establishment there. 'I had no scope for my own initiative,' wrote Mabell. 'My position as the wife of the head of the family was not recognized.'

Finally, the Victorian preoccupation with rituals of bereavement and death also affected the social round. When in deep mourning, ladies withdrew from society. Close relatives would normally suspend their customary activities for at least a year, although for lesser categories of mourning three months might suffice. During the first year after her husband's death, a widow would wear a black dress covered with crape and a widow's cap with a veil. Second mourning lasted for the next twelve months and comprised black with less crape, without the cap and with jet ornaments. During the third year half-mourning might be worn, with grey or mauve added for colour. However, reactions to widowhood varied between individuals. Lady Dalmeny displayed a firm practical sense when in August 1854, less than four years after her husband's death, she married the elderly but rich Lord Harry Vane, later the 4th Duke of Cleveland. This ended her financial worries and enabled her to re-enter society as a brilliant, if sometimes intimidating, hostess.

CHAPTER 4

Mistress of the Household

One of the prime responsibilities of the Victorian lady after marriage was the efficient management of her household. Wives were expected not merely to create a comfortable home but to uphold their husband's social position by the high quality of the hospitality they offered. This covered the food and drink that were served, the entertainment provided at dinner parties and other events, and the splendour of the furnishings and ornaments that adorned the house's principal rooms. It was the desire to indicate wealth and status through possessions that led to the cluttered appearance of so many Victorian homes.

However, a successful hostess needed special skills, not least in putting guests at ease. Lady Ponsonby was described by her daughter as an excellent *maîtresse de maison*. Her food was famous and under her tuition 'any cook became a star'. She even wrote a cookery book that was much in demand, and a cook who had been in her service had little difficulty in getting a fresh place.

In achieving this kind of success, however, much depended on the recruitment of good staff. As *The Servant's Practical Guide* (1880) put it: 'Without the constant co-operation of well-trained servants, domestic machinery is completely thrown out of gear, and the best bred of hostesses placed at a disadvantage.' In aristocratic households, that might mean the employment of twenty or more domestics (including both male and female); but in upper-middle-class homes three or four, usually female, servants would be the norm. Butlers and footmen were considered more prestigious than parlour maids because of the higher wages they commanded and their more specialised duties. One lady, when establishing new social connections in London, declared that she would not pay calls on any household that 'only had a parlour maid'.

Mrs Beeton compared the mistress of a household to the commander of an army. As such, she must offer leadership to her domestic employees. 'Her spirit will be seen through the whole establishment . . . just in proportion as she performs her duties intelligently and thoroughly, so will her domestics follow in her path.' To this end regular visits should be made to the kitchen and other offices, while she should arrange for the purchase of provisions herself or, if she has a housekeeper to carry out that task, she should examine the woman's accounts frequently. A household account book must be kept and bills settled promptly.

The exercising of these financial controls was something many ladies found difficult, especially in the early years of marriage. 'Housekeeping looks alarming when I see the bills,' wrote Lady Amberley to her sister after less than five months of married life: '£11 the first week for the grocer − £3 for the butcher alone without fish and poultry . . . & I have been under the impression we were living on so little.' Two days later she reported that she had spoken to the cook about the bills: '7 lbs of butter in one week, I did not scold but she dissolved into tears. She says she cannot do with less meat than we had last week & we had three fowls & twice fish besides & 8 quarts of milk in a week.' Lady Frederick Cavendish, too, found her 'house-books . . . came to a heavy total', when she first began to balance them. Less than a year after marriage she also encountered difficulties with the servants − an experience she shared with many Victorian ladies. On 17 May, 1865, she lamented: 'a new chapter of household cares: viz., failures. The kitchen-maid turns out sick and incapable; the upperhousemaid pert, fine, and lazy. Woe is me!' She also had the 'miserable catastrophe' of a housekeeper who drank and a series of lady's maids who quarrelled with the other servants.

Part of the problem was that otherwise conscientious mistresses often failed to follow Mrs Beeton's strictures on the need for constant vigilance. Even experienced wives like Marion Sambourne, who ran an upper-middle-class home in Kensington with four female servants and a groom, rarely went to the kitchen. Instead she gave orders to the cook in the morning room. Gwen Raverat's mother adopted a still more distant approach to most aspects of domestic life. According to her daughter:

> Ladies were ladies in those days; they did not do things themselves, they told other people what to do and how to do it. My mother would have told anybody how to do anything: the cook how to skin a rabbit, or the groom how to harness a horse; though of course she had never done . . . these operations herself.

Consequently, the maids largely ran the Raverat household, although they showed tact in taking account of their mistress's foibles and economies. For example, the mistress objected to the use of lard, but the cook always had plenty of it on hand. As Gwen commented drily, it was probably 'called by some other name in the account book – and it was safe, for my mother would not have recognized the stuff if she had seen it on the kitchen table'. The household stores were locked in a cupboard and were doled out as needed, but the maids soon learned to ask for more than they required at any one time, so as to build up stocks for the future. On other occasions they indicated a shortage, for instance of sugar, by ensuring that the sugar-basin in the dining room was left empty.

These casual methods on the part of mistresses encouraged petty theft, with provisions such as tea and sugar, which were not likely to be missed, secretly passed on to friends or relatives. Buyers of kitchen waste would also contact cooks, offering to buy on liberal terms their perquisites of dripping and other fat. This encouraged deception, with candles stolen to add weight to the mixture, or butter purloined to supplement legitimate perquisites. Elsewhere, as at Hesleyside in Northumberland, Barbara Charlton was shocked to discover that the butler and his friends regaled themselves with wine at the family's expense, while they themselves often drank water with their dinner. There were also clandestine sexual encounters involving some of the servants. Years later Mrs Charlton claimed that the laundry was 'nothing but a brothel', although she did not make clear to whom the laundry maids offered their favours. Such disclosures would certainly have been condemned by Mrs Beeton and her fellow writers on household management as indications of laxity in a mistress's own system of control.

In the largest households, where there were numerous servants working in different departments, there were other difficulties to resolve. At Blenheim Palace, where there were over thirty indoor servants in the late 1890s, the Duchess of Marlborough remembered the clashes between some department heads.

They included rows between the French chef and the housekeeper over the provision of breakfast trays, since meat dishes were cooked in the kitchen while other items were prepared in the still-room by the house-keeper and her staff. Unfortunately 'the kitchen and still-room were separated by yards . . . of damp, unheated passages so that the food was often cold'. Similar disagreements occurred between the chef and the butler, and it was the Duchess's task to eliminate these frictions since they could have jeopardised the culinary success of her dinner parties.

As in other major establishments the Duchess also cooperated with the housekeeper over the allocation of bedrooms for the many house parties that were held. In 1892 Lady Greville compared large country houses to popular hostelries, with people arriving and departing every day. This was a considerable responsibility for the mistress and her senior domestics. 'Her head must be a perfect encyclopaedia, with its varied and always ready knowledge,' wrote Lady Greville. She must 'never forget, never be ruffled, never be "caught napping"'. Yet all trace of household cares must vanish when she donned her evening gown and sat 'bediamonded at the head of her table'. There she must appear 'the impersonation of pleasure and gaiety'.

For reasons of prestige as well as hospitality, great care was taken to provide a lavish array of dishes when preparing menus for dinner parties. That applied even in relatively modest households. Marion Sambourne kept a small notebook in which she recorded dinner party menus, both her own and those of other people, as well as recipes. Thus a dinner for eight she served on 18 June 1880 comprised: 'Kippered cod's roe, capers, bread and butter. Julienne soup. Cold trout, sauce piquante. Pigeons with asparagus. Forequarters of lamb, mint sauce, tomato salad, potatoes. Beans aux francais. Ducklings, green peas. Coffee savoy, plum tart, cream. Anchovies, parmesan cheese, etc.'

Such an ambitious bill of fare required much work and a good deal of skill on the part of the cook.

Although temporary helpers were hired to assist the parlour maid in serving the meal, there is no mention of additional staff in the kitchen, or that Marion herself lent a hand. She did, however, carry out some special shopping for dinner parties, such as purchasing crayfish and cherries, although the basic necessities were ordered by the cook. Marion merely paid the 'books' from time to time.

Perhaps not surprisingly, Mrs Sambourne was often worried about temperamental cooks who 'had to be replaced at short notice', to say nothing of idle housemaids who failed to meet her rigorous standards for daily cleaning and polishing. She herself might do a little dusting in the drawing room if she thought it was needed and would wash delicate china ornaments herself. But like most ladies, these domestic chores were undertaken spasmodically. More regular were the shopping expeditions she and many other upper-middle-class wives carried out to buy household utensils. In larger establishments, that would be the responsibility of the housekeeper or butler, unless the mistress especially reserved the task to herself.

Some wives, however, even in country houses, were actively involved in the day-to-day running of their home, rather than delegating this to servants. Lady Elizabeth Shiffner, who lived at Hamsey in Sussex, hired and fired the domestics, paid their wages and kept a record of recipes for anything from cowslip wine and plum cake to furniture polish and medicaments. She prepared inventories of the linen and china in the house and noted the produce from the home farm. She entered cheese- and butter-making competitions, and retained some of the proceeds from the retail sale of produce for her personal use. Maggie Wyndham, too, took over some of the domestic responsibilities at Petworth in 1898, when her mother, Lady Leconfield, was away. The duties undertaken included the selection of carpeting for the servants' hall and the purchase of ingredients for a Christmas cake. Often in these large households, essential provisions were purchased in bulk once or twice a year from a trusted supplier, with 'extras' secured when needed.

Alongside the management of domestic staff and the provision of meals for family and guests, there were other matters to concern the mistress of a Victorian household. These included the heating of rooms, since many large properties were extremely cold during the winter. Even with coal fires in every room, the long unheated corridors and the substantial area to be warmed meant that these houses could be very uncomfortable. At Eaton, on the outskirts of Chester, Lady Elizabeth Grosvenor found the huge vaulted rooms and unheated corridors so icy that she wore voluminous flannel underwear, put on two pairs of stockings and had wash leather insteps to protect her legs against the cold. Marion Sambourne's diaries, too, contain entries to the effect that her husband's bath water was frozen or that she had had to keep her shawl on all night because she was so cold. The Sambournes economised by rarely having fires in their bedroom.

Hygiene issues caused anxieties as well. They ranged from the eradication of bedbugs, perhaps brought into the house with the laundry, if this were sent out, to the dangers of bad drains. Jeannette Marshall, daughter of a London surgeon, commented on 'greenwater smells' when she visited the homes of some of her friends, and her mother carried eau de cologne to ward off unpleasant odours. Marion Sambourne blamed the washbasin in her bedroom for the sore throats she suffered.

A desire to keep kitchen smells from penetrating to the main rooms of the house led early Victorian architects to keep kitchen and dining room far apart – a practice that made for cold food and much labour in carrying dishes to the dining table. Only in the last years of the nineteenth century did the practice come under question, with the two rooms brought into greater proximity, 'to economize on labour'.

In the days before refrigeration it was difficult, especially in town households, to prevent food from going bad. Although the Sambournes had a patent form of icebox, Marion complained of 'Bad mutton at lunch' or that they had had a 'Very late dinner, duck bad, had to send out for lobster and steak'. In large properties plentiful supplies of ice were brought in and there were big larders in which meat and game could be stored. Even so, preserving food remained a problem.

Finally, in the case of mistresses of country houses, there were the moves of family and servants from one property to another to oversee, where several estates were owned, or the transfer from the country to the town in readiness for the London Season. Although domestic staff carried out the manual tasks associated with this, the mistress had to ensure they carried out their duties efficiently. As the obituarist of Harriet Duchess of Sutherland commented after her death in 1868: 'The ordering of a very large establishment indoors and out of doors must always be a true test of the right understanding of her duties towards her household by the Lady at their head.'

CHAPTER 5

The Role of 'Lady Bountiful'

The dispensing of charity was an integral part of many Victorian ladies' lives. It was regarded as an extension of the traditional female 'nurturing' role, although it also offered women a means of escape from the limitations of much of their everyday domestic experience. It enabled them to demonstrate their organisational abilities, to show their own personality, and to gain satisfaction from their achievements. It gave them a chance, too, of exercising power over the lives of others through the decisions they took to provide assistance to the old, the sick and the needy.

For most country house wives and daughters it was a duty associated with their rank and, as such, was expected of them by the villagers living in and around the family estate. In 1892 Lady Greville described the lady of the manor as

> the supreme dispenser of tea, soup, flannel, and advice . . . Not a bazaar can be organized without her patronage and aid; not a charitable committee held, not a church restored . . . unless it be graced with her presence and glorified by her support . . . Every case of distress is duly reported to her . . . The soup-kitchen during the cold winter months, the labourers' Christmas dinners, the tenants' feast . . . the school-children's tea, the new year's treat, all have to be arranged for and purveyed from her department.

Sometimes the women concerned found the expectations hard to satisfy. In November 1843 Cecilia Ridley distributed clothing and other articles to the residents of Plessey in Northumberland, near her

Blagdon home. These were supplied through a club she organised, but, as she commented drily, whenever she went to Plessey she was 'obliged to make a visit to all the people or they are quite jealous. They stand at their doors and call me in, and they begin "Well Hinny" and tell me all their wants and ailments.'

On occasion housekeepers lent a hand if the lady of the manor was unable to carry out the duties herself. In 1839, when the Countess of Carnarvon was in Italy with her husband, their long-serving housekeeper, Mrs Goymour, arranged for the distribution of bags of baby linen, which were lent to poor families in the neighbourhood of Highclere Castle. She also alerted the Countess to the need for replacements, as many articles were worn out. Similarly, in December 1896 the housekeeper at Blenheim Palace helped the Duchess of Marlborough and her sisters-in-law to pack up bundles of clothing and other items for the Duchess to hand over as Christmas gifts on her visits to estate families.

Even wives and daughters lower down the social scale attended charitable bazaars and other fundraising events, and supplied food and clothing to the needy. They made goods for sales-of-work and, especially in the towns, went into the homes not only of the 'respectable' poor but also of those leading squalid and disreputable lives. They went into workhouses to read to the inmates and visited orphanages, where they provided little 'extras' for the children. They taught in schools as volunteers – especially in Sunday schools but in ordinary day classes as well; they paid the school fees of some of the poorest pupils; and they provided treats and prizes. In March 1870 Catharine Paget, daughter of a leading London medical man, began teaching arithmetic to 'a largish class of infants' at the Burlington School, under the auspices of her parish church, St James's, Piccadilly. As she noted in her diary, she hoped that if she made mistakes 'nobody was the worse'. She also commenced visiting 'poor people' and participated in meetings of the district committee which co-ordinated these activities. Such ventures were undertaken alongside a very full social life, but it is clear that she saw them as 'work' and as a manifestation of her strong Christian faith.

For other women, religion and a desire to 'do good' led to intervention in even more difficult areas, such as visiting prisons and brothels, this last undertaken in an attempt to rescue the prostitutes. One volunteer was Sarah Robinson, whose initial foray into brothels in Aldershot proved a testing experience. She paced up and down outside the building, praying for strength, before dashing inside. 'Most of the girls were not up; nearly all, after their first surprise, received me kindly . . . I could not write down, I cannot even bear to think of the horrible things I saw and heard.' When she got home she was violently sick, but she persisted with her mission, aided by two assistants. They prayed and sang outside while she went to talk to the girls. She was reported to have 'rescued' five to ten girls a week, taking them to a refuge.

Some Victorian ladies saw philanthropy as a bridge between their own privileged lives and those of the poor. That was true of Lady Frederick Cavendish, whose religious faith, coupled with the encouragement and example of her aunt, Catherine Gladstone, led to her taking up various charitable causes in London from the 1860s. In February 1866, for example, she became a volunteer teacher at a school associated with St Martin's Church but clearly found it an ordeal. She confessed to being taken aback 'by the coolness and talkativeness of my pale-faced cockney damsels who were very ready to put me in the right way. The row was great and my numbers unmanageable, so I did not make a satisfactory start.' What the pupils gained from these interventions by untrained upper-class instructors is not clear. There seems to have been a hope that their ladylike demeanour and good manners would provide a role model for the youngsters and would serve to reduce class tensions.

A few days after her first teaching experience Lady Frederick drove with Mrs Gladstone to visit the

London Hospital, where they 'talked and read to divers poor men and some poor little children; then to the workhouse'. This was St George's-in-the-East workhouse, which she had agreed to visit fortnightly. 'I am to have a ward of decrepit old men, who enjoyed some peppermints I brought.' After this expedition she lunched at Devonshire House but felt uneasy about the contrast between the luxury she was enjoying there and the poverty she had witnessed earlier. 'I hope it is not wrongly selfish to feel refreshed by one's comforts and pleasant refined things after going a little into the depths. One knows the poor people do not crave for *these* things, and one has been trying to cheer them; still, it feels selfish.'

Two decades later the young Margaret Gladstone was similarly inspired by a strong religious desire to 'do good'. She organised boys' clubs in Kensington associated with the church she attended, as well as teaching at a domestic servant training school, and on Easter Sunday 1889, aged 19, she took her first Sunday school class. During the 1890s she became a school manager and in December 1892 became involved with the Hoxton and Haggerston District Nursing Association, of which she later became secretary. This supplied domiciliary nursing care to the poor of the district, and Margaret also visited some of the patients. In that same year she joined the Charity Organisation Society, which pioneered casework methods in dealing with poor families and sought to end indiscriminate almsgiving. Instead, its aim was to give comprehensive aid designed to make families self-dependent. By that date, however, she was moving away from purely philanthropic work and was turning to political reform. This led to involvement with the Women's Industrial Council and the National Union of Women Workers, both of which sought to raise the social and economic status of female employees. In 1896, after her marriage to MacDonald, Margaret joined the Independent Labour Party – something that few Victorian gentlewomen did. But alongside these political interests she

retained her strong Christian faith and her commit-
ment to the welfare of the poor.

Where the role of 'Lady Bountiful' was carried
through sympathetically, as with Margaret Gladstone, it
created warm bonds between donor and recipient and
made acceptable the patriarchal social system it
bolstered. But not all providers displayed sensitivity.
Thus Lady Wilbraham, daughter of the Earl of
Fortescue, on most Saturdays drove round the cottages
on her husband's Cheshire estate in a pony carriage,
dispensing 'various gifts such as red flannel, soup,
puddings, etc. and the basket nearly always contained a
bottle of castor oil which was frequently administered,
to the consternation of the recipients'. Similarly, the
Countess of Warwick remembered that although her
mother and stepfather were

good to the poor . . . it was always a goodness of
extreme condescension. On matters of faith, politics,
education and hygiene, they were convinced that

those who served had no right to an opinion . . . [A]
measure of serfdom prevailed . . . in the surroundings
of every country house I ever visited . . . Blankets,
soup, coals, rabbits, and the rest were all paid for . . .
not in cash . . . but in subservience.

Occasionally this meant that cottagers who failed to
display the expected signs of gratitude and deference
would be reproved, or perhaps penalised by the with-
drawal of aid.

Even in the countryside, however, old-style indiscriminate philanthropy came under question during
the Victorian years. Patrons sought to encourage
sobriety, piety and self-reliance by sponsoring coal and
clothing clubs, friendly societies and medical charities,
which they partly financed but to which prospective
recipients of the benefits were expected to subscribe.
Educational schemes, too, were promoted and steps
taken to improve the employment prospects of young
people, especially the girls, by introducing training for

domestic service or by seeking posts for would-be maids in the households of acquaintances. Anne Sturges Bourne of Eling, Hampshire, was one such. As she told a friend in November 1853: 'Getting places & people to fit is one of the chief employments of life.' In the early 1850s she started a servants' training school in her own house and described rather enviously a similar institution set up by the Duchess of Sutherland. This had forty girls boarded, lodged and trained, '& she gets them places – very well for a fine lady. But I wd. not have 40 girls if I could . . . I think the only reason mine have done well . . . is that they are few & like a family & can be studied individually.' In 1861 Anne had eight children in training at her home, the oldest aged 14 and the youngest 10. All except one had been born in the vicinity of Eling.

But it was not just the recipients who benefited from these initiatives. Particularly for spinsters, who lacked the social status that went with being married, philanthropy offered an outlet for their energies and ideas.

Their skill in advising, planning, organising and publicising their chosen causes gave them self-confidence and self-esteem. This was true of unmarried gentlewomen such as Anne Sturges Bourne and Alice Balfour. The latter found the limitations of her domestic circumstances deeply frustrating, but was able to deploy her considerable administrative talents by founding a Nursing Association in East London in 1898 to train nurses. She also interested herself in the welfare of tenants on the family estate. As with Catharine Paget, this was seen as 'work', at a time when on social grounds such women were precluded from pursuing a recognised profession.

Many ladies enjoyed their contacts with the families they befriended. The Duchess of Marlborough, trapped in a loveless marriage, found consolation in her visits to the almshouses in Woodstock, where there were 'old ladies whose complaints had to be heard and whose infirmities had to be cared for, and there were the blind to be read to. There was one gentle, patient old lady whom I loved . . . I grew to know the Gospel of St John by heart because it was her favourite . . . I felt the peace of God descending into that humble home and I was happy to go there.'

For a number of women, however, the desire to 'do good' was combined with a wish to enjoy the social aspects of philanthropy. For the ambitious nouveaux riches charity could provide a means of extending the range of their acquaintances and of making contact with those of superior rank. For others it offered companionship and entertainment. Gwen Raverat remembered how the ladies of Cambridge enjoyed their committees, and another critic described the Dorcas meetings held by ladies in his parish, to make clothes for the poor, as excuses for gossip, 'only relieved by tea and buttered toast'. For younger women, sales-of-work and bazaars provided entertainment and an opportunity to shine. Maud Tomlinson, who lived with elderly parents on the Isle of Wight, noted that she and her closest friend went to a bazaar in July 1889, 'wearing the new white dresses we have copied out of *The Ladies' Pictorial* . . . The Bazaar quite a success. Our guitar duet was well received.' The previous year they had worn fancy dress, with Maud and another friend 'rushed off our feet, providing tea and refreshments for the teeming hordes who attended . . . Both of us were dressed as national flags . . . I wore the French tricolour . . . Several customers for tea mistook me for a French girl and addressed me in that language', much to her amusement.

It was such events that led Leonore Davidoff to note the 'interlocking of "Society" and charity . . . Charity Bazaars, Fancy Fairs, private theatricals, charity garden parties (which were also occasions to show off private homes) were used as money-raising functions to support charitable purposes. But for many people they were seen primarily as part of the season's social calendar.'

CHAPTER 6

Pleasures, Pastimes and Other Pursuits

Many of the pleasures and pastimes of Victorian ladies were associated with their general social round. These included the dinner parties, balls, concerts, plays and sporting events they attended, as well as the lengthy stays they made in country houses and the homes of relatives. But there were quiet domestic amusements as well, such as embroidery, the playing of cards, the assembling of scrapbooks and albums of pressed flowers, the writing of letters, sketching and reading. 'A taste for drawing must . . . be ranked among the elegances of social life,' declared *All About Etiquette* (*c.* 1879), adding that while musical skill was 'a pleasant acquirement', it was 'not a sufficient substitute for an acquaintance with general literature'. Nevertheless, it conceded that musical evenings at home could provide a pleasing diversion for the whole family. Needlework was part of the evening's recreation for many of the 'ladies of the household . . . varied by an occasional game at chess or backgammon'. It had also 'often been remarked . . . that nothing [was] more delightful to the feminine members of a family than the reading aloud of some good standard work or amusing publication'.

Religion played an important role in many women's lives, with private devotions supplemented by frequent attendance at services and other events associated with the church. Marion Bradley, the wife of a master at Rugby School who later became headmaster of Marlborough College, wrote extensively in her diary about her inner spiritual life and her own short-comings. She described pregnancy as 'a heavy burden and trial', and in September 1855, when expecting her third child, confessed to hardly knowing how to bear 'this state of uneasiness of body & mind. I feel so irritable that I know not how often I lose controul [sic] over my temper. I am incapable of finding enjoyment in any thing, incapable of reading even the Bible – & long to fly from myself.' Her baby was born the following November.

Catharine Paget was also deeply religious, sometimes attending two or three services in a day, in addition to her Sabbath devotions. She often commented on the merits of the sermons she heard.

Gardening was a common activity for many Victorian gentlewomen, and although the hard physical labour was normally carried out by paid male workers, the planning of a garden's layout and the carrying out of a little weeding or the dead-heading of flowers were pastimes they enjoyed. Lady Dorothy Nevill recalled proudly that when she and her husband moved to the Dangstein estate on the borders of Hampshire in the mid-nineteenth century she devoted much time to the garden. 'We had seventeen hot-houses . . . Most of the tropical fruit trees were there as well as orchids without number.'

Younger women and wives of limited means engaged in dressmaking and in the trimming of hats and bonnets, either to update clothes that had become unfashionable or to extend their wardrobe at modest cost. Jeannette Marshall was anxious to be better dressed than the annual £12 or so pocket and glove money she received from her parents would permit. As a consequence she spent, on average, over 3 hours a day, year in year out, during the 1870s and 1880s (including holiday periods) making or remaking dresses and bonnets, trimming hats and sewing underclothes. By so doing she probably saved an outlay of about £35 a year. However, her parents continued to pay for her main wardrobe even when she was in her late twenties.

Jeannette, like many Victorian ladies living in towns, spent a good deal of time going round the shops. The weekday walks undertaken by herself, her mother and her sister normally combined exercise with shopping expeditions. According to her biographer, a day on which she did not make purchases was an exception, despite her straitened finances. Catharine Paget, too, frequently walked to the principal London shops, chaperoned by her mother or her brother. She was far better off than Jeannette Marshall, having an annual allowance of £50, as well as receiving additional funds. Some of her purchases were consequently quite expensive, as in January 1871 when she spent £1 5s on a muff and collar, 15s 6d on a scarlet skirt, £1 1s on a ball dress, and 11s on gloves, among other things. On 4 January she turned down an opportunity to go ice-skating with her friends (a favourite winter activity) so that she and her mother could go to Marshall & Snelgrove's sale. This was one of the capital's more exclusive drapers. In all, between 1 January and 2 April 1871, she spent £16 4s 6d on clothes, presents for friends or family members, and gifts to the church or to charity.

For those less fortunate, lack of cash could hamper many activities for unmarried girls, such as attending classes in singing, dancing and drawing. Maud Tomlinson on the Isle of Wight wanted to have drawing lessons, but in July 1888 ruefully concluded her father would consider it a waste of money. She herself had only £1 12s in her 'Penny Box'. Not until February 1891 did she persuade her parents to let her learn 'from a live artist. Have made a special painting smock out of a pair of old brown linen curtains. Bought three painting brushes and a palette with which I hope to essay great things.'

Women's participation in sport increased over the period, with croquet and archery popular in the 1860s and lawn tennis from the mid-1870s, despite the cumbersome clothes females wore. In the 1880s Maud Tomlinson and her friends were enthusiastic tennis players and regularly entered tournaments. They also enjoyed occasional ladies' cricket matches. But the new tennis craze did not meet with approval from all contemporaries, and especially condemned was its popularity at garden parties. In 1877 *Sylvia's Home Journal* noted there was truth in a critic's comment that 'women taking an active part in a lawn-tennis competition may be compared to a swan waddling on a bowling green, for women clad in the dresses of the present day were never intended by Providence to run'. Over time the clothes worn for tennis became lighter and freer, but even in 1893 Lady Colin Campbell advised that dresses should be of wool 'as a preventive of chills being taken', while a 'receptacle for the tennis balls is sometimes part of the player's costume'.

During the 1890s cycling gave a new liberty to women and at least one Victorian lady considered that travelling around her home town had been 'transformed by the iron machine. I fly about . . . with the greatest of ease, greeting friends with a nonchalant wave of the hand . . . To think I wasted all my youth on trains and in cabs when there was this alternative.'

Affluent gentlewomen, such as the widowed Emily Meynell Ingram of Temple Newsam in Yorkshire, might own a yacht. For eleven years from 1886 she and a few friends spent two or three months twice a year cruising in the Mediterranean during the spring and in Scandinavia or the Baltic during the summer. They commemorated the journeys with witty poems, watercolours and photographs inserted in the yacht's log books. Other ladies, such as the Countess of Warwick and Lucy Lyttelton, enjoyed hunting. In January 1862, on a country house visit to Newnham Paddox, Lucy described a day out with the local pack as

delightful and memorable . . . I saw the fox break away, I heard the music of the hounds, and horns and halloos, I careered along to the sound of the scampering hoofs . . . I flew over 2 or 3 fences, too enchanted to have a moment's fright . . . I think it was the most glorious exciting enjoyment I have ever had.

Holidays at the coast gave younger women especially the opportunity to bathe in the sea and undertake long hikes. In the summer of 1870 Catharine Paget went with her family and friends for a lengthy stay in Wales. During the visit she climbed to the top of Snowdon, an achievement she proudly recorded in her diary. On another occasion, she, her sister and a friend had a 'capital bathe in a good rough sea', before she went out sketching. In the afternoon they had a 'great walk ... to the top of Penmaenmawr'.

Many affluent families spent holidays on the Continent, especially in France and Italy, although Switzerland increased in popularity during the later nineteenth century, both for winter sports and for summer vacations for those who appreciated the beauties of the natural landscape. Jeannette Marshall and her parents and sister visited Switzerland more than once in the 1870s. But Jeannette was less concerned with the scenery than with seizing the opportunity of the more relaxed hotel environment to flirt with men to whom she had not been formally introduced, in a way that would have been frowned upon in London.

A few women from professional families went on foreign tours organised by travel agents like Thomas Cook, from the mid-1850s. These escorted trips enabled females to visit places where it would have been impossible for them to go on their own. As Matilda Lincolne from Norwich commented in the 1850s, many friends had thought she and her three sisters were 'too independent and adventurous' in going off in this fashion without a 'protecting relative'. But the fact that they were in a group led by Thomas Cook himself had calmed fears. She urged other unattached ladies to follow their example.

Alongside these pleasures and pastimes, however, a small minority of Victorian gentlewomen were anxious to engage in serious academic pursuits, in the second half of the nineteenth century, perhaps studying on courses arranged by the University Extension movement. From the late 1860s a few attended the new women's colleges attached to Oxford and Cambridge Universities. Louisa Lumsden, for example, in 1868 found release from the 'balls and croquet without end' in Scottish polite society by attending lectures for women given in Edinburgh by university professors. Through these she was able to attend what became Girton College, Cambridge, to pursue more rigorous studies. But friends tried to dissuade her mother from letting her go, believing it would mean her 'social extinction'. Similarly, when Lady Cynthia Asquith expressed a wish to go to college her parents firmly vetoed the suggestion, declaring that to be associated with a university education 'would undoubtedly be a scandal it would take many seasons to live down'. Opposition to women's higher education rested on the belief that such intellectual aspirations were inappropriate for a lady and would damage both her health and her marital prospects. She would be classed as an unglamorous, uninteresting 'blue-stocking'. Nonetheless, a growing number of ladies did take up this academic option, and by the early 1880s it was accepted in some circles that females should have access to advanced education, albeit only so they would become more intellectually capable wives and mothers – not career women. Hence Jane Harrison, later a well-known archaeologist, recalled how, when she was absorbed in studying a Greek grammar book, a favourite aunt declared plaintively: 'I do not see how Greek grammar is to help little Jane keep house when she has a home of her own.'

Similar reservations attended women's efforts to widen their involvement in politics beyond that of hostess, entertaining the leading figures in their chosen party and acting as confidantes for up-and-coming Members of Parliament. Only a small minority of Victorian ladies wanted parliamentary suffrage to be extended to women on the same terms as men's suffrage. In 1867 Lady Frederick Cavendish condemned the idea as 'odious and ridiculous' and expressed alarm that it was beginning to be spoken of without laughter. She and her sisters held those anti-suffrage views to the end of the century. Yet that did not prevent her from electioneering on her husband's behalf at the 1880 general election, when he stood as a Liberal candidate. Other women, too, canvassed on behalf of their menfolk at general elections. Constance Flower, for example, despite great nervousness, took an active part in the 1880 election at Brecon and had the satisfaction of seeing her husband elected – as Lady Frederick also did.

However, some women were more ambitious and seized the chance to make a personal political contribution in the sphere of local government. From 1870 women could stand for election to the newly created school boards, which were designed to supplement the existing system of voluntary elementary education. They could also become poor law guardians, dispensing parish relief to the old and the needy, from 1875. In 1894 the creation of parish and district councils gave them the opportunity to be elected to these bodies as well. In January 1895 the *Parish, District and Town Councils' Gazette* reported approvingly that one of the most 'pleasing features of the recent elections' had been the 'comparatively large numbers of lady members of the Aristocracy who [had] been chosen to take a share either as Councillors or Chairmen in the government of the villages where their family estates [were] situated'.

For some gentlewomen these political activities were linked to previous charitable commitments. Miss Martha Merrington, the first female poor law guardian, was elected for Kensington in 1875, but she had already established crèches there and wished to extend her welfare interests. Similarly, Edith Cropper's desire 'to make the workhouse children's lives a little sweeter' impelled her to seek election as a poor law guardian. There were many similar examples.

Finally, from 1883 women acquired another means of showing support for their favoured political party without standing for election themselves, by becoming members of auxiliary organisations associated with them. These trained supporters to act as unpaid election campaign workers. The first of them, and by far the most successful, was the Primrose League, set up by the Conservatives in 1883, and recruiting women members on equal terms to men a year later. By 1891 the League had around half a million female supporters, who distributed leaflets and posters, raised funds and canvassed voters at election time. In Gloucestershire, for example, Lady Hicks-Beach made sure voters were registered, and lent carriages at elections to take them to the polls. Lord Henniker's daughter, Mary, sponsored nine Primrose League branches (or habitations, as they were called) within the Eye constituency alone, and nine more elsewhere in Suffolk. For many ladies the League enabled them to demonstrate their organisational skills and political awareness, while their high social status meant they could appear in public in this way without losing caste. Meresia Nevill, Lady Dorothy's daughter, claimed, indeed, that they made the best canvassers because of their previous philanthropic experience in visiting the homes of the sick and needy.

In 1886 the Liberal Party responded to the Conservative challenge with its own Women's Federation. By the mid-1890s it had around 80,000 members, and under the influence of the Countess of Carlisle, who became its President in 1893, it espoused the cause of female suffrage. This led some Federation members to break away but the Countess was unmoved. She strongly supported Irish Home Rule, as well as the temperance cause, and was elected a district councillor in 1895. She and the Earl closed several licensed premises on their estates and opened reading rooms instead. She also started cooperative societies around their Yorkshire and Cumberland properties and promoted smallholdings and allotments. One daughter described her as 'an Olympian', whose presence 'in the house was diffused through a priesthood of governesses, tutors and head maids'.

Very few Victorian ladies were as politically committed – or as self-willed – as the Countess of Carlisle. Most obeyed the injunction of *The Primrose Magazine* of August 1887 that women should not 'set . . . themselves up in the place of men' but should 'rather work for good, quietly, having . . . gentle sympathy and general charity of heart to all concerned'. This unobtrusive role was their appropriate sphere.

For the rest, much of the time of Victorian gentlewomen was spent within the circle of their immediate family and friends, dealing with domestic matters and carrying out the duties and enjoying the recreations associated with this. Some followed Lady Cardigan's example of wifely devotion. When she found her husband enjoyed only riding, driving and walking, she 'naturally . . . put [her] own hobbies aside and entered into all his favourite pursuits'. But by the end of the nineteenth century most ladies had become sufficiently self-assured to reject such a derivative approach.